Software Testing Series
Security Testing

Written by:
Michael Pasono
Volume 1 – 2024

Contents

Overview

About the Author

Michael Pasono, CISSP is the author behind _Software Testing Series – Security Testing_ which underscores the importance of protecting your company data during software development processes as threat-actors continue to look for and enumerate paths in software applications/APIs and those related software vulnerabilities.

Michael's professional experience and advocacy in systems quality improvement, cybersecurity, and data protection has him recognized as an industry leader in researching technology innovations and assuring high quality systems.

Michael shares key best practices and recommends approaches to protect your data throughout the entire software requirements, design, pre-deployment, and deployment processes.

The recommendations are provided by Michael himself and not any paid sponsors or partners. We hope you take these best practices and implement them into your processes to reduce risk of losing your valuable data and/or impacting your company brand.

Why Important and Preamble

Security testing is crucial during software development for <u>several reasons</u>:

Identifying Vulnerabilities

Security testing helps in uncovering vulnerabilities and weaknesses in the software. By simulating real-world attack scenarios, security testing helps discover potential entry points for malicious actors.

Risk Mitigation

Detecting and addressing security issues early in the development process reduces the overall risk of security breaches. This proactive approach is more cost-effective than fixing vulnerabilities after the software has been deployed.

Compliance Requirements

Many industries and regulatory bodies have specific security and privacy requirements that software must adhere to. Security testing ensures that the software complies with these standards, preventing legal and financial consequences.

Protecting User Data

In today's digital age, protecting user data is of utmost importance. Security testing ensures that sensitive information, such as personal details and financial data, is adequately safeguarded against unauthorized access.

Maintaining Reputation

Security breaches can significantly damage the reputation of a company or product. Conducting thorough security testing helps in building trust among users and stakeholders, as it demonstrates a commitment to delivering secure and reliable software.

Preventing Financial Loss

Security incidents can lead to financial losses through legal actions, compensation, and the costs associated with fixing and recovering from a breach. Security testing minimizes the likelihood of such financial repercussions.

Ensuring Business Continuity

Security testing contributes to the overall resilience of a system. By identifying and addressing vulnerabilities, it helps ensure that the software functions as intended, even in the face of potential security threats.

Staying Ahead of Evolving Threats

The threat landscape is constantly evolving, with new attack vectors and techniques emerging regularly. Security testing helps organizations stay ahead of these threats by continuously assessing and adapting security measures.

Avoiding Downtime

Security incidents can lead to system downtime, disrupting business operations. Through security testing, organizations can identify and address vulnerabilities that might otherwise result in service interruptions.

Promoting a Security Culture

Incorporating security testing into the development process fosters a culture of security awareness among development teams. This mindset encourages proactive consideration of security implications at every stage of the software development lifecycle.

In summary, security testing is an integral part of software development that goes beyond mere compliance. It is a proactive and strategic approach to safeguarding systems, data, and user trust in an increasingly interconnected and digital world.

Companies

Companies are capitalizing on collecting as much data as they can about their potential and current customers and it's beginning to shine a light into data privacy rights for the average person. With companies collecting so much data, they must hire security experts **and testers** to keep this data safe to assure their brand reputation. Companies do this collection because they realize your data turns into revenue for them and shareholders.

Hacker Attack Methods

Hackers exploit vulnerabilities in software that has not been properly developed and tested through various techniques. Here are some common ways hackers may attack inadequately tested software:

Injection Attacks

SQL Injection (SQLi)

Attackers manipulate input fields to inject malicious SQL queries, potentially gaining unauthorized access to databases.

Cross-Site Scripting (XSS)

Hackers inject malicious scripts into web pages, which are then executed by users' browsers, enabling the theft of sensitive information.

Insecure Direct Object References (IDOR)

Exploiting improper access controls, hackers can manipulate input to access unauthorized data or resources.

Security Misconfigurations

Default settings, unnecessary services, and open ports may expose vulnerabilities. Hackers exploit these misconfigurations to gain unauthorized access.

Brute Force Attacks

Unprotected authentication mechanisms are susceptible to brute force attacks, where hackers repeatedly attempt to guess usernames and passwords.

Buffer Overflow Attacks

Poorly validated input may lead to buffer overflow vulnerabilities, allowing attackers to execute arbitrary code by overflowing the allocated memory space.

Zero-Day Exploits

Hackers target unknown vulnerabilities (zero-days) for which no patches or fixes exist. Inadequately tested software may have undiscovered vulnerabilities that hackers exploit before developers can address them.

File Inclusion Exploits

Insecure file inclusion mechanisms may allow attackers to execute arbitrary code by including files with malicious content.

Denial of Service (DoS) and Distributed Denial of Service (DDoS)

Software with inadequate resilience may succumb to DoS attacks, overwhelming servers with traffic and causing service disruptions.

Man-in-the-Middle (MitM) Attacks

Insecure communication channels may allow hackers to intercept and manipulate data between two parties without detection.

Security Token Exploitation

Insecure handling of session tokens or authentication tokens may enable attackers to impersonate users.

Inadequate Data Validation

Insufficient validation of user input may lead to data manipulation attacks, such as command injection or XML External Entity (XXE) attacks.

Phishing Attacks

Inadequately tested software may lack robust mechanisms to detect and prevent phishing attempts, putting users at risk of identity theft or credential compromise.

Race Conditions

Flaws in concurrent processing may allow attackers to manipulate the sequence of operations, leading to unauthorized access or data corruption.

Social Engineering

Human factors, such as weak password policies or lack of user awareness, can be exploited through social engineering tactics to gain unauthorized access.

To mitigate these risks, thorough security testing, including penetration testing, code reviews, and vulnerability assessments, is essential. Regular updates, patches, and adherence to secure coding practices can significantly reduce the likelihood of successful attacks on software systems.

Further reference

The creation of this book is in partnership with Apply QA, LLC; a leading provider of best practices and consultation services for software quality assurance best practices. In fact, the founder and CEO of this company is Michael himself.

Please visit https://www.applyqa.com to check out their educational products and services.

Chapter 1 – Understand the Development Cycle

Overview

Software development typically follows a structured or formal process known as the Software Development Life Cycle (SDLC). The SDLC consists of several phases, each with its own set of activities and goals.

Most companies today develop following agile processes such as Kanban, Scrum, SAFe, etc. The main goal of being "agile" is you can make quick feature changes into production.

Knowing how long it takes to properly test software (including security), having an automated testing practice is a necessity.

Typical Phases of SDLC

Requirements Gathering

In this phase, stakeholders, including clients and end-users, communicate their needs and expectations. Requirements are documented to outline the functionalities and features the software should have.

Planning

Project planning involves defining project scope, timelines, resource allocation, and budgeting. A project plan outlines the tasks, milestones, and dependencies for the entire development process.

Design

The design phase translates the requirements into a detailed system architecture. This includes high-level design (system architecture) and low-level design (detailed specifications for components/modules).

Implementation (Coding)

Developers write code based on the design specifications. This phase involves actual programming and creating the software according to the established design.

Testing

The software is tested to ensure that it meets the specified requirements and works as intended. Testing includes unit testing, integration testing, system testing, and user acceptance testing.

Deployment

The software is deployed to a production environment for end-users to access. This phase involves activities such as data migration, user training, and ensuring that the system is ready for live use.

Maintenance and Support

After deployment, the software enters the maintenance phase. This involves fixing bugs, addressing issues, and providing ongoing support. Updates and enhancements may also be introduced based on user feedback or changing requirements.

Chapter 2 – When does security testing start?

Far Left
(Requirements)

Far left stands for shifting whatever process you need in quality engineering to increase your return on investment (ROI).

Think about the standard software testing process. If you wait to do actual testing or skip testing as a whole and you find a bug in production, the cost to fix is exponentially bigger (up to 100x) than if a developer ran the appropriate test in let's say Unit Testing phase of the SDLC.

The reasoning is because you typically have a lot of change controls and developer changes such as doing branching and merging. It gets even more costly if you are limited by your non-production environment.

Now you might be thinking, well how do I do "security testing" in a requirements phase? Isn't that just getting the business requirements so we know how to design and build? The answer is no.

Proper quality engineering practices have evolved into the requirements phase. For now, we will just focus on security testing, but it applies to many other forms of testing.

Once you understand what business is asking for in terms of features, it's time to think about non-functional features. These would be features that still need to be tested such as performance, scalability, usability, and **security**.

Consider security requirements during the gathering phase. Define and document security specifications based on the identified risks and the nature of the software being developed.

Consider what technical architecture is needed to meet the features your end user is looking for. Make sure you work with the architects to assess known vulnerabilities or attack methods before design/build phase. This can be as simple as a checklist of technologies, capabilities, and risks known in the wild.

If you see a known risk, talk with the architect or engineer assigned to mitigate before even starting design/build phase.

Along with this review, make sure you are keeping this checklist updated as new vulnerabilities are released. Best to set up a good vulnerability management program and integrate.

Design, Build, Code Phase

Now that you have reviewed the technology picked to start building the solution, it's time to start thinking about threat modeling and risk analysis.

Conduct threat modeling and risk analysis during the design phase. Identify potential security threats and vulnerabilities in the system architecture. Design security controls and mechanisms to mitigate these risks.

Apply secure coding practices during the implementation phase. Developers should follow best practices for input validation, use secure APIs, and avoid common security pitfalls. Code reviews with a focus on security should be performed regularly.

Provide educational resources to your developers on how to properly code for following these secure coding practices.

Make sure you also include these resources for any new developers that join your team.

Testing Phases

Now that your developers should be following the best practices for secure code, its time to make sure the test strategy plan outlines the proper scope and depth of security testing needed. Integrate the following types of security testing.

If your team has just started doing security testing, note that using integrated and **automated security tools related to these types of tests is recommended.** The overhead of manually scanning code can be intense.

Static Application Security Testing (SAST)

Analyzing the source code for vulnerabilities without executing the program.

Dynamic Application Security Testing (DAST)

Evaluating the security of a running application by simulating real-world attacks.

Penetration Testing

Employing ethical hacking techniques to identify vulnerabilities and weaknesses.

Security Scanning

Using automated tools to scan for known vulnerabilities in dependencies and configurations.

My recommendation as mentioned before, is to make sure that the **automated tools you are using for these types of tests is with a reputable vendor that keeps versions updated** frequently against CVE's and other known attack paths as in Hacker Attack Methods section of this book.

It is **industry practice to also look to the outside vendors to conduct penetration or vulnerability scans on a routine basis** if your team doesn't have the expertise or funding to support. Sometimes it's cheaper to use a vendor that specializes in this type of test.

CI/CD Pipelines

CI/CD pipelines are all about building automated and quickly reusable software builds to push new features faster into production. Obviously, this has most security professionals concerned with a miss in a known vulnerability.

Implement security checks in the CI/CD pipeline to **ensure that security testing is an integral part of the automated build and deployment process.** Automated security tests can help catch issues early in the development cycle.

If your team is integrating a new third-party vendor/API, make sure the proper security testing is done.

The first time you execute these security scans in your automated pipeline might cause a lot of alerts or code reviews so please keep that in mind when deploying a new product or feature the 1st time but once you get the initial scans done, reoccurring scans should give fewer and fewer alerts if following the best practices outlined.

Before you move to PROD

While most of your security scanning and fixes should be complete, it's also a best practice to have another eye on it.

If you are part of a large company, this might be a dedicated security team that should conduct a more formal security assessment or penetration test to make sure your processes align with enterprise best practices.

Once you get this approval from another person or department, it's time to go live into production. Follow your typical deployment process.

Post-Deployment (Monitoring)

Implement continuous monitoring for security threats and vulnerabilities in the production environment. Regularly update and patch the software to address newly discovered security issues.

While this doesn't fit under the realm of security testing, it's important to have a process that monitors and informs the development team of security changes needed.

Chapter 3 - Static - SAST

Tooling and Setup

Select a SAST Tool

Choose a SAST tool that best fits your organization's needs, budget, and programming languages used in your software projects.

Some popular SAST tools include:

- Fortify Static Code Analyzer
- Checkmarx
- Veracode Static Analysis
- SonarQube (with appropriate plugins)

Install or Configure the SAST Tool

Install the chosen SAST tool on your development environment or set it up to integrate with your existing development infrastructure. Follow the installation instructions provided by the tool's documentation.

Integrate with Version Control Systems (VCS)

Integrate the SAST tool with your version control system (e.g., Git, SVN) to analyze code directly from the repository. This enables automated scanning of code during the development process.

Configure the tool to trigger scans automatically whenever new code is committed or pushed to the repository.

Configure Build Automation Tools

Integrate the SAST tool with your build automation tools (e.g., Jenkins, Azure Pipelines, CircleCI) to incorporate security scans into your continuous integration (CI) and continuous deployment (CD) pipelines.

Configure the build scripts or pipelines to execute SAST scans as part of the automated build process.

Customize Scan Policies

Customize scan policies based on your organization's security requirements and coding standards. Define rulesets and thresholds for identifying security vulnerabilities, coding flaws, and compliance violations.

Fine-tune scan configurations to reduce false positives and focus on critical issues that require immediate attention.

Schedule Regular Scans

Schedule regular SAST scans to analyze the entire codebase or specific code repositories at predefined intervals (e.g., daily, weekly). Regular scanning helps identify security issues early in the development lifecycle.

Review and Interpret Results

Review the results of SAST scans to identify security vulnerabilities, potential threats, and areas of improvement in the codebase.

Prioritize identified issues based on severity, impact, and likelihood of exploitation. Collaborate with developers to remediate security findings and address underlying vulnerabilities.

Provide Developer Training and Support

Offer training sessions and resources to developers on secure coding practices, common security vulnerabilities, and how to interpret SAST findings effectively.

Provide support and guidance to developers in addressing security issues identified during SAST scans, including code refactoring and implementing secure coding techniques.

Monitor and Track Progress

Monitor the progress of SAST initiatives by tracking the number of vulnerabilities detected, resolved, and mitigated over time.

Continuously refine and improve SAST processes based on feedback, emerging threats, and changes in the software development landscape.

Chapter 4 - Dynamic - DAST

Tooling and Setup

Select a DAST Tool

Choose a DAST tool that aligns with your organization's requirements, including supported technologies, scalability, and reporting capabilities.

Some popular DAST tools include:

- Burp Suite
- OWASP ZAP (Zed Attack Proxy)
- Netsparker
- Acunetix

Install or Configure the DAST Tool

Install the chosen DAST tool on your testing environment or set it up to integrate with your existing infrastructure.

Configure the tool's settings, including authentication mechanisms, crawling depth, and scan policies, based on your application's architecture and security requirements.

Configure Authentication and Session Management

Configure the DAST tool to handle authentication and session management mechanisms used by your web application.

Provide credentials or configure authentication workflows to ensure that the tool can access restricted areas of the application during testing.

Define Target Application(s)

Define the target application(s) or URLs that you want to test using the DAST tool.

Specify the scope of the test, including specific endpoints, parameters, and input fields to be scanned.

Configure Scan Settings

Customize scan settings and parameters based on your testing objectives and risk tolerance.

Adjust scan options such as scan depth, crawl settings, input vectors, and attack payloads to maximize coverage and identify potential vulnerabilities effectively.

Schedule and Execute Scans

Schedule regular DAST scans to assess the security posture of your web applications proactively.

Execute scans manually or automate them as part of your continuous integration (CI) and continuous deployment (CD) pipelines to integrate security testing into the development lifecycle.

Analyze Scan Results

Analyze the results of DAST scans to identify security vulnerabilities, including common web application vulnerabilities such as SQL injection, cross-site scripting (XSS), and insecure authentication mechanisms.

Prioritize identified vulnerabilities based on severity, impact, and likelihood of exploitation.

Interpret Findings and Remediate Vulnerabilities

Interpret the findings from DAST scans and collaborate with development teams to remediate identified vulnerabilities.

Provide guidance and recommendations on secure coding practices, input validation, output encoding, and other measures to mitigate security risks.

Integrate with Issue Tracking Systems

Integrate the DAST tool with your issue tracking system (e.g., Jira, Bugzilla) to create and manage security findings as actionable tickets.

Track the status of vulnerabilities, assign tasks to relevant stakeholders, and monitor progress towards resolution.

Retest and Validate Fixes

Retest the web application after applying fixes to validate that vulnerabilities have been addressed effectively.

Conduct regression testing to ensure that security patches do not introduce new vulnerabilities or regressions.

Continuous Improvement

Continuously refine and improve your DAST testing practices based on feedback, lessons learned, and emerging threats.

Stay informed about new attack vectors, security trends, and best practices to enhance the effectiveness of your DAST program.

Chapter 5 – Penetration Testing

Internal to your company

Define Scope and Objectives

Determine the scope of the internal penetration testing, including the systems, networks, and applications to be assessed.

Define the objectives of the testing, such as identifying vulnerabilities, assessing security controls, and measuring the effectiveness of defensive mechanisms.

Select Testing Team

Assemble a team of skilled security professionals or engage certified penetration testing experts to conduct the internal assessment.

Ensure that the testing team has access to the necessary tools, resources, and permissions to perform the tests effectively.

Gain Stakeholder Buy-In

Obtain approval and support from relevant stakeholders, including IT management, system administrators, and business owners, for conducting internal penetration testing activities.

Conduct Testing

Execute the penetration testing activities according to the predefined scope and objectives.

Use a variety of techniques and tools to simulate real-world attack scenarios, including network scanning, vulnerability assessment, exploitation, privilege escalation, and lateral movement.

Document Findings

Document all findings, including identified vulnerabilities, weaknesses, and areas of concern.

Classify and prioritize vulnerabilities based on severity, impact, and likelihood of exploitation.

Remediation and Follow-Up

Collaborate with system owners and stakeholders to remediate identified vulnerabilities and address security gaps.

Provide recommendations and guidance on implementing effective security controls and mitigating risks.

Conduct follow-up assessments to verify the effectiveness of remediation efforts and ensure ongoing security improvement.

<u>Continuous Education</u>

Have your team practice and keep up to date by doing capture the flag (CTF) events and encourage healthy competition within the team. There is numerous capture the flag external vendors to research & review.

Many of the sites offer either free or paid subscriptions. If you have a larger team, investigate an enterprise license to help save costs for your employees.

Be sure to look for machines that are added more frequently and target newer vulnerabilities found.

External (Vendor)

Vendor Selection

Evaluate and select a reputable penetration testing vendor with expertise in conducting external assessments across various industries and technology domains.

Consider factors such as vendor experience, qualifications, certifications, methodologies, and reputation in the industry.

Define Scope and Requirements

Clearly define the scope of the external penetration testing engagement, including the external-facing systems, applications, and infrastructure to be assessed.

Specify the testing requirements, objectives, timelines, and deliverables in the engagement contract or statement of work (SOW).

Engage Vendor

Establish communication channels and engage with the selected vendor to discuss project requirements, expectations, and logistics.

Provide necessary access credentials, network diagrams, and documentation to facilitate the testing process.

Perform Testing

Allow the penetration testing vendor to conduct external assessments using a combination of automated scanning tools, manual testing techniques, and specialized methodologies.

Monitor the testing activities and coordinate with the vendor to address any issues or challenges that may arise during the engagement.

Review Findings

Review the findings and reports provided by the penetration testing vendor, including identified vulnerabilities, exploit scenarios, and recommended remediation measures.

Validate the accuracy and relevance of the findings through discussions with the vendor and internal security teams.

Remediate Vulnerabilities

Take prompt action to remediate identified vulnerabilities and security weaknesses in the external infrastructure and applications.

Implement security patches, configuration changes, and controls to mitigate risks and enhance the overall security posture.

Continuous Improvement

Incorporate lessons learned from the external penetration testing engagement into your organization's security policies, procedures, and practices.

Establish a culture of continuous improvement by conducting regular assessments, monitoring security trends, and adapting security measures to evolving threats.

Chapter 6 – Vulnerability Scanning, Auditing, and Monitoring

Scanning

Vulnerability Scanning

Conduct regular vulnerability scans using automated scanning tools such as **Nessus, OpenVAS, or Qualys**.

These tools identify known vulnerabilities in network devices, servers, operating systems, and applications by comparing them against databases of known security flaws.

Auditing

Configuration Auditing

Perform configuration audits to ensure that systems and applications are securely configured according to best practices and industry standards.

Tools like **CIS Benchmarks and Microsoft Baseline Security Analyzer (MBSA)** can help assess configuration settings and identify deviations from recommended security guidelines.

With the **evolution of using cloud, misconfigurations are a top risk** for companies. It's best to implement an automated scanning tool to review configurations in your cloud environment.

Monitoring

Log Analysis and Monitoring

Implement centralized logging and monitoring solutions to collect, analyze, and correlate security events and logs from various sources across the IT infrastructure.

Tools such as **Splunk, ELK Stack (Elasticsearch, Logstash, Kibana), and Security Information and Event Management (SIEM) platforms** help detect suspicious activities, anomalies, and security incidents in real-time.

Since the scope of this book is around security software testing, the following proactive security controls will not be included.

The other proactive cybersecurity controls (outside of security software testing) are using Web Application Firewalls (WAF), File Integrity Monitoring (FIM), Network Intrusion Detection and Prevention Systems (IDS/IPS), Endpoints, Patch Management, Hygiene Assessments, and Third-Party Risk Management.

Chapter 7 – Cloud Shift

Overview

With most companies now using cloud for software development and integrations to on-prem, it is critical to understand the architecture and what your company owns compared to what the cloud provider owns in relation to risk.

There will be a **progression of what assets your company currently owns to what is now owned by the cloud provider.**

The shift for software security testing is learning more about these contracts and **making sure you are testing what you NEED too**, knowing that cloud providers might be taking some of that responsibility.

Use cloud-specific security testing tools and services to assess security controls, configurations, and compliance posture of cloud resources, such as AWS Inspector, Azure Security Center, and GCP Security Command Center.

API Security

Test the security of cloud-based APIs and web services to ensure authentication, authorization, input validation, and data protection mechanisms are implemented securely.

Chapter 8 – Cloud Security Process and Tools Setup

Overview

Setting up tools for cloud security testing involves selecting appropriate tools, configuring them to align with your cloud environment, and integrating them into your security testing processes.

Implementing Processes and Tools

Assess Requirements

Understand your organization's cloud environment, including the cloud service provider(s) you use (e.g., AWS, Azure, GCP), types of services deployed (e.g., IaaS, PaaS, SaaS), and the specific security challenges and requirements you need to address.

Select Cloud Security Testing Tools

Research and evaluate cloud security testing tools that are compatible with your cloud environment and meet your organization's requirements.

Consider factors such as supported cloud platforms, integration capabilities, scanning features, reporting capabilities, scalability, and cost.

Choose Tool Categories

Identify the types of cloud security testing tools you need based on your security testing objectives and requirements. Common categories of cloud security testing tools include:

Vulnerability Management

Tools for identifying and remediating vulnerabilities in cloud infrastructure, applications, and configurations.

Configuration Management

Tools for assessing and enforcing secure configurations and compliance policies in cloud environments.

Threat Detection and Incident Response: Tools for monitoring, detecting, and responding to security threats and incidents in cloud-based assets.

Compliance and Governance

Tools for ensuring compliance with regulatory requirements, industry standards, and cloud provider security guidelines.

Integrate with Cloud Providers

Integrate the selected cloud security testing tools with your cloud provider's management console or API endpoints to enable seamless interaction and data exchange.

You should configure access credentials, permissions, and authentication mechanisms to establish secure connections and authenticate tool access to your cloud environment.

Configure Scanning Policies

Define scanning policies, rulesets, and parameters based on security best practices, regulatory requirements, and organizational security policies.

Customize scanning configurations, thresholds, and frequency settings to align with your organization's risk tolerance and security objectives.

Implement Continuous Monitoring

Set up continuous monitoring capabilities to monitor your cloud environment for security threats, vulnerabilities, and compliance violations in real-time.

Configure alerts, notifications, and automated responses to trigger actions in response to security events and incidents detected by the monitoring tools.

Automate Security Testing Workflows

Automate security testing workflows and processes by integrating cloud security testing tools with your existing DevOps toolchain, CI/CD pipelines, and automation frameworks.

Implement automated testing, scanning, and remediation tasks to streamline security operations and reduce manual effort.

Establish Reporting and Analytics

Configure reporting and analytics features in your cloud security testing tools to generate comprehensive reports, dashboards, and visualizations of security findings, trends, and metrics.

Customize report templates, export options, and sharing mechanisms to communicate security insights effectively with stakeholders and decision-makers.

Train and Educate Users

Provide training and educational resources to security teams, cloud administrators, developers, and other stakeholders on how to use the cloud security testing tools effectively.

Offer guidance on interpreting security findings, prioritizing remediation efforts, and implementing security best practices in cloud environments.

Monitor Tool Performance

Monitor the performance and effectiveness of cloud security testing tools in identifying and mitigating security risks over time.

Track key performance indicators (KPIs), metrics, and trends related to vulnerability management, compliance status, incident response, and security posture improvement.

Evaluate and Adapt

Regularly evaluate the effectiveness and suitability of the cloud security testing tools deployed in your environment.

Solicit feedback from users, conduct periodic assessments, and review tool capabilities to identify areas for improvement and adaptation.

Chapter 9 – Security Testing AI/ML

Overview

Security testing for AI/ML (Artificial Intelligence/Machine Learning) systems involves assessing the security risks associated with the data, algorithms, models, and infrastructure used in AI/ML applications.

Types of Security Testing

Data Security Testing

Assess the security of data used to train and test AI/ML models. Evaluate data integrity, confidentiality, and privacy to ensure sensitive information is adequately protected.

Test data sources for potential vulnerabilities, such as injection attacks, data poisoning, and adversarial examples.

Implement data anonymization, encryption, access controls, and data loss prevention (DLP) measures to protect sensitive data throughout its lifecycle.

Model Security Testing

Evaluate the security of AI/ML models to identify vulnerabilities and adversarial attacks that could compromise their integrity or performance.

Conduct model analysis, including sensitivity analysis, model inversion attacks, and model extraction attacks, to assess the robustness and resilience of AI/ML models against adversarial manipulation.

Test model inputs for evasion attacks, adversarial perturbations, and input manipulation techniques that could bypass detection mechanisms and lead to incorrect predictions or decisions.

Algorithm Security Testing

Review the security of algorithms and techniques used in AI/ML systems, including machine learning algorithms, deep learning architectures, and reinforcement learning algorithms.

Assess algorithmic bias, fairness, and transparency to ensure that AI/ML models do not discriminate against protected groups or exhibit unethical behavior.

Test algorithms for resilience against algorithmic manipulation, poisoning attacks, and model inversion attacks that exploit vulnerabilities in algorithmic decision-making processes.

Infrastructure Security Testing

Evaluate the security of the infrastructure and environment used to develop, train, deploy, and operate AI/ML systems.

Conduct vulnerability assessments and penetration testing of cloud-based platforms, containerized environments, APIs, and microservices architecture used to support AI/ML workflows.

Implement secure development practices, container security measures, and network segmentation to prevent unauthorized access, data breaches, and denial-of-service (DoS) attacks against AI/ML infrastructure.

Adversarial Testing

Perform adversarial testing to identify and exploit weaknesses in AI/ML systems from an adversarial perspective.

Employ adversarial machine learning techniques, such as adversarial examples, evasion attacks, and model extraction attacks, to evaluate the robustness and resilience of AI/ML models against sophisticated adversaries.

Use adversarial testing frameworks and libraries to generate adversarial samples and evaluate the effectiveness of defense mechanisms and mitigation strategies.

Compliance and Governance Testing

Ensure compliance with regulatory requirements, industry standards, and ethical guidelines governing the development and deployment of AI/ML systems.

Conduct audits, risk assessments, and compliance checks to verify adherence to data protection laws, privacy regulations, and ethical principles in AI/ML applications.

Implement governance frameworks, transparency measures, and accountability mechanisms to promote responsible AI/ML development and mitigate potential risks to stakeholders and society.

Continuous Monitoring and Incident Response

Establish continuous monitoring capabilities to detect anomalous behavior, security incidents, and unauthorized activities in AI/ML systems.

Implement anomaly detection algorithms, behavior analytics, and threat intelligence feeds to monitor AI/ML workflows and infrastructure for signs of compromise or suspicious behavior.

Conclusion

By incorporating security testing at each stage of the software development process, organizations can create a more secure software product, reduce the likelihood of security incidents, and build trust with users and stakeholders.

It's essential to view security as an ongoing and integral part of the development lifecycle rather than a separate, isolated activity.

With the advancement in data collection techniques and bots scanning all servers attached to the internet, along with artificial intelligence machines connecting multiple datasets to make sense of the data, it is important to keep security testing and monitoring at the forefront of each development project you have.

My hope is that you get some insight and best practices into how you can improve your software development lifecycle (SDLC) to help secure a better tomorrow.